THE WANDERER
His Parables and His Sayings

THE BOOKS OF
KAHLIL GIBRAN

"His power came from some great reservoir of spiritual life else it could not have been so universal and so potent, but the majesty and beauty of the language with which he clothed it were all his own."   CLAUDE BRAGDON

•••

Beloved Prophet: The Love Letters of
Kahlil Gibran and Mary Haskel
Edited by Virginia Hilu
This Man from Lebanon: A Study of
Kahlil Gibran *by Barbara Young*

PUBLISHED BY ALFRED A. KNOPF

THE WANDERER
His Parables and His Sayings

BY

Kahlil Gibran

1983

NEW YORK : ALFRED·A·KNOPF

CONTENTS

THE WANDERER

His Parables and His Sayings

*The seven illustrations in this volume
are reproduced from original drawings
by the author*

THE WANDERER

I met him at the crossroads, a man with but a cloak and a staff, and a veil of pain upon his face. And we greeted one another, and I said to him, " Come to my house and be my guest."

And he came.

My wife and my children met us at the threshold, and he smiled at them, and they loved his coming.

Then we all sat together at the board and we were happy with the man for there was a silence and a mystery in him.

And after supper we gathered to the fire and I asked him about his wanderings.

He told us many a tale that night and also the next day, but what I now record was born out of the bitterness of his days though he himself was kindly, and these tales are of the dust and patience of his road.

And when he left us after three days we did not feel that a guest had departed but rather that one of us was still out in the garden and had not yet come in.

GARMENTS

Upon a day Beauty and Ugliness met on the shore of a sea. And they said to one another, " Let us bathe in the sea."

Then they disrobed and swam in the waters. And after a while Ugliness came back to shore and garmented himself with the garments of Beauty and walked his way.

And Beauty too came out of the sea, and found not her raiment, and she was too shy to be naked, therefore she dressed herself with the raiment of Ugliness. And Beauty walked her way.

And to this very day men and women mistake the one for the other.

Yet some there are who have beheld the face of Beauty, and they know her notwithstanding her garments. And some there be who know the face of Ugliness, and the cloth conceals him not from their eyes.

THE EAGLE AND THE SKYLARK

A skylark and an eagle met on a rock upon a high hill. The skylark said, " Good morrow to you, Sir." And the eagle looked down upon him and said faintly, " Good morrow."

And the skylark said, " I hope all things are well with you, Sir."

" Aye," said the eagle, " all is well with us. But do you not know that we are the king of birds, and that you shall not address us before we ourselves have spoken? "

Said the skylark, " Methinks we are of the same family."

The eagle looked upon him with disdain and he said, " Who ever has said that you and I are of the same family? "

Then said the skylark, " But I would remind you of this, I can fly even as high as you, and I can sing and give delight to the other creatures

6

of this earth. And you give neither pleasure nor delight."

Then the eagle was angered, and he said, "Pleasure and delight! You little presumptuous creature! With one thrust of my beak I could destroy you. You are but the size of my foot."

Then the skylark flew up and alighted upon the back of the eagle and began to pick at his feathers. The eagle was annoyed, and he flew swift and high that he might rid himself of the little bird. But he failed to do so. At last he dropped back to that very rock upon the high hill, more fretted than ever, with the little creature still upon his back, and cursing the fate of the hour.

Now at that moment a small turtle came by and laughed at the sight, and laughed so hard that she almost turned upon her back.

And the eagle looked down upon the turtle and he said, "You slow creeping thing, ever one with the earth, what are you laughing at?"

And the turtle said, "Why I see that you are

turned horse, and that you have a small bird riding you, but the small bird is the better bird."

And the eagle said to her, " Go you about your business. This is a family affair between my brother, the lark, and myself."

THE LOVE SONG

A poet once wrote a love song and it was beautiful. And he made many copies of it, and sent them to his friends and his acquaintances, both men and women, and even to a young woman whom he had met but once, who lived beyond the mountains.

And in a day or two a messenger came from the young woman bringing a letter. And in the letter she said, " Let me assure you, I am deeply touched by the love song that you have written to me. Come now, and see my father and my mother, and we shall make arrangements for the betrothal."

And the poet answered the letter, and he said to her, " My friend, it was but a song of love out of a poet's heart, sung by every man to every woman."

And she wrote again to him saying, " Hypocrite and liar in words! From this day unto my coffin-day I shall hate all poets for your sake."

TEARS AND LAUGHTER

Upon the bank of the Nile at eventide, a hyena met a crocodile and they stopped and greeted one another.

The hyena spoke and said, " How goes the day with you, Sir? "

And the crocodile answered saying, " It goes badly with me. Sometimes in my pain and sorrow I weep, and then the creatures always say, ' They are but crocodile tears.' And this wounds me beyond all telling."

Then the hyena said, " You speak of your pain and your sorrow, but think of me also, for a moment. I gaze at the beauty of the world, its wonders and its miracles, and out of sheer joy I laugh even as the day laughs. And then the people of the jungle say, ' It is but the laughter of a hyena.' "

AT THE FAIR

There came to the Fair a girl from the country-side, most comely. There was a lily and a rose in her face. There was sunset in her hair, and dawn smiled upon her lips.

No sooner did the lovely stranger appear in their sight than the young men sought her and surrounded her. One would dance with her, and another would cut a cake in her honor. And they all desired to kiss her cheek. For after all, was it not the Fair?

But the girl was shocked and startled, and she thought ill of the young men. She rebuked them, and she even struck one or two of them in the face. Then she ran away from them.

And on her way home that evening she was saying in her heart, " I am disgusted. How un-mannerly and ill bred are these men. It is beyond all patience."

A year passed during which that very comely

girl thought much of Fairs and men. Then she came again to the Fair with the lily and the rose in her face, the sunset in her hair and the smile of dawn upon her lips.

But now the young men, seeing her, turned from her. And all the day long she was unsought and alone.

And at eventide as she walked the road toward her home she cried in her heart, " I am disgusted. How unmannerly and ill bred are these youths. It is beyond all patience."

THE TWO PRINCESSES

In the city of Shawakis lived a prince, and he was loved by everyone, men and women and children. Even the animals of the field came unto him in greeting.

But all the people said that his wife, the princess, loved him not; nay, that she even hated him.

And upon a day the princess of a neighboring city came to visit the princess of Shawakis. And they sat and talked together, and their words led to their husbands.

And the princess of Shawakis said with passion, " I envy you your happiness with the prince, your husband, though you have been married these many years. I hate my husband. He belongs not to me alone, and I am indeed a woman most unhappy."

Then the visiting princess gazed at her and said, " My friend, the truth is that you love your husband. Aye, and you still have for him a passion unspent, and that is life in woman like unto Spring in a garden. But pity me, and my husband, for we do but endure one another in silent patience. And yet you and others deem this happiness."

THE LIGHTNING FLASH

There was a Christian bishop in his cathedral on a stormy day, and an un-Christian woman came and stood before him, and she said, " I am not a Christian. Is there salvation for me from hell-fire? "

And the bishop looked upon the woman, and he answered her saying, " Nay, there is salvation for those only who are baptized of water and of the spirit."

And even as he spoke a bolt from the sky fell with thunder upon the cathedral and it was filled with fire.

And the men of the city came running, and they saved the woman, but the bishop was consumed, food of the fire.

THE HERMIT AND THE BEASTS

Once there lived among the green hills a hermit. He was pure of spirit and white of heart. And all the animals of the land and all the fowls of the air came to him in pairs and he spoke unto them. They heard him gladly, and they would gather near unto him, and would not go until nightfall, when he would send them away, entrusting them to the wind and the woods with his blessing.

Upon an evening as he was speaking of love, a leopard raised her head and said to the hermit, " You speak to us of loving. Tell us, Sir, where is your mate? "

And the hermit said, " I have no mate."

Then a great cry of surprise rose from the company of beasts and fowls, and they began to say among themselves, " How can he tell us of loving and mating when he himself knows naught thereof? " And quietly and in disdain they left him alone.

That night the hermit lay upon his mat with his face earthward, and he wept bitterly and beat his hands upon his breast.

THE PROPHET
AND THE CHILD

Once on a day the prophet Sharia met a child in a garden. The child ran to him and said, "Good morrow to you, Sir," and the prophet said, "Good morrow to you, Sir." And in a moment, "I see that you are alone."

Then the child said, in laughter and delight, "It took a long time to lose my nurse. She thinks I am behind those hedges; but can't you see that I am here?" Then he gazed at the prophet's face and spoke again. "You are alone, too. What did you do with your nurse?"

The prophet answered and said, "Ah, that is a different thing. In very truth I cannot lose her oftentimes. But now, when I came into this garden, she was seeking after me behind the hedges."

The child clapped his hands and cried out, "So you are lost like me! Isn't it good to be lost?" And then he said, "Who are you?"

And the man answered, " They call me the prophet Sharia. And tell me, who are you? "

" I am only myself," said the child, " and my nurse is seeking after me, and she does not know where I am."

Then the prophet gazed into space saying, " I too have escaped my nurse for awhile, but she will find me out."

And the child said, " I know mine will find me out too."

At that moment a woman's voice was heard calling the child's name. " See," said the child, " I told you she would be finding me."

And at the same moment another voice was heard, " Where art thou, Sharia? "

And the prophet said, " See, my child, they have found me also."

And turning his face upward, Sharia answered, " Here am I."

THE PEARL

Said one oyster to a neighboring oyster, " I have a very great pain within me. It is heavy and round and I am in distress."

And the other oyster replied with haughty complacence, " Praise be to the heavens and to the sea, I have no pain within me. I am well and whole both within and without."

At that moment a crab was passing by and heard the two oysters, and he said to the one who was well and whole both within and without, " Yes, you are well and whole; but the pain that your neighbor bears is a pearl of exceeding beauty."

BODY AND SOUL

A man and a woman sat by a window that opened upon Spring. They sat close one unto the other. And the woman said, " I love you. You are handsome, and you are rich, and you are always well-attired."

And the man said, " I love you. You are a beautiful thought, a thing too apart to hold in the hand, and a song in my dreaming."

But the woman turned from him in anger, and she said, " Sir, please leave me now. I am not a thought, and I am not a thing that passes in your dreams. I am a woman. I would have you desire me, a wife, and the mother of unborn children."

And they parted.

And the man was saying in his heart, " Behold another dream is even now turned into the mist."

And the woman was saying, " Well, what of a man who turns me into a mist and a dream? "

THE KING

The people of the Kingdom of Sadik surrounded the palace of their king shouting in rebellion against him. And he came down the steps of the palace carrying his crown in one hand and his sceptre in the other. The majesty of his appearance silenced the multitude, and he stood before them and said, " My friends, who are no longer my subjects, here I yield my crown and sceptre unto you. I would be one of you. I am only one man, but as a man I would work together with you that our lot may be made better. There is no need for a king. Let us go therefore to the fields and the vineyards and labor hand with hand. Only you must tell me to what field or vineyard I should go. All of you now are king."

And the people marveled, and stillness was upon them, for the king whom they had deemed the source of their discontent now yielded his crown and sceptre to them and became as one of them.

Then each and every one of them went his way, and the king walked with one man to a field.

But the Kingdom of Sadik fared not better without a king, and the mist of discontent was still upon the land. The people cried out in the market places saying that they would be governed, and that they would have a king to rule them. And the elders and the youths said as if with one voice, " We will have our king."

And they sought the king and found him toiling in the field, and they brought him to his seat, and yielded unto him his crown and his sceptre. And they said, " Now rule us, with might and with justice."

And he said, " I will indeed rule you with might, and may the gods of the heaven and the earth help me that I may also rule with justice."

Now, there came to his presence men and women and spoke unto him of a baron who mistreated them, and to whom they were but serfs. And straightway the king brought the baron

23

before him and said, " The life of one man is as weighty in the scales of God as the life of another. And because you know not how to weigh the lives of those who work in your fields and your vineyards, you are banished, and you shall leave this kingdom forever."

The following day came another company to the king and spoke of the cruelty of a countess beyond the hills, and how she brought them down to misery. Instantly the countess was brought to court, and the king sentenced her also to banishment, saying, " Those who till our fields and care for our vineyards are nobler than we who eat the bread they prepare and drink the wine of their wine-press. And because you know not this, you shall leave this land and be afar from this kingdom."

Then came men and women who said that the bishop made them bring stones and hew the stones for the cathedral, yet he gave them naught, though they knew the bishop's coffer was full of gold and silver while they themselves were empty with hunger.

24

And the king called for the bishop, and when the bishop came the king spoke and said unto him, "That cross you wear upon your bosom should mean giving life unto life. But you have taken life from life and you have given none. Therefore you shall leave this kingdom never to return."

Thus each day for a full moon men and women came to the king to tell him of the burdens laid upon them. And each and every day for a full moon some oppressor was exiled from the land.

And the people of Sadik were amazed, and there was cheer in their heart.

And upon a day the elders and the youths came and surrounded the tower of the king and called for him. And he came down holding his crown with one hand and his sceptre with the other.

And he spoke unto them and said, " Now, what would you of me? Behold, I yield back to you that which you desired me to hold."

But they cried, " Nay, nay, you are our rightful king. You have made clean the land of vipers, and you have brought the wolves to naught, and we come to sing our thanksgiving unto you. The crown is yours in majesty and the sceptre is yours in glory."

Then the king said, " Not I, not I. You yourselves are king. When you deemed me weak and a misruler, you yourselves were weak and misruling. And now the land fares well because it is in your will. I am but a thought in the mind of you all, and I exist not save in your actions. There is no such person as governor. Only the governed exist to govern themselves."

And the king re-entered his tower with his crown and his sceptre. And the elders and the youths went their various ways and they were content.

And each and every one thought of himself as king with a crown in one hand and a sceptre in the other.

UPON THE SAND

Said one man to another, " At the high tide of the sea, long ago, with the point of my staff I wrote a line upon the sand; and the people still pause to read it, and they are careful that naught shall erase it."

And the other man said, " And I too wrote a line upon the sand, but it was at low tide, and the waves of the vast sea washed it away. But tell me, what did you write? "

And the first man answered and said, " I wrote this: ' I am he who is.' But what did you write? "

And the other man said, " This I wrote: ' I am but a drop of this great ocean.' "

THE THREE GIFTS

Once in the city of Becharrè there lived a gracious prince who was loved and honored by all his subjects.

But there was one exceedingly poor man who was bitter against the prince, and who wagged continually a pestilent tongue in his dispraise.

The prince knew this, yet he was patient.

But at last he bethought him; and upon a wintry night there came to the door of the man a servant of the prince, bearing a sack of flour, a bag of soap and a cone of sugar.

And the servant said, " The prince sends you these gifts in token of remembrance."

The man was elated, for he thought the gifts were an homage from the prince. And in his pride he went to the bishop and told him what the prince had done, saying, " Can you not see how the prince desires my goodwill? "

But the bishop said, " Oh, how wise a prince,

and how little you understand. He speaks in symbols. The flour is for your empty stomach; the soap is for your dirty hide; and the sugar is to sweeten your bitter tongue."

From that day forward the man became shy even of himself. His hatred of the prince was greater than ever, and even more he hated the bishop who had revealed the prince unto him.

But thereafter he kept silent.

PEACE AND WAR

Three dogs were basking in the sun and conversing.

The first dog said dreamily, " It is indeed wondrous to be living in this day of dogdom. Consider the ease with which we travel under the sea, upon the earth and even in the sky. And meditate for a moment upon the inventions brought forth for the comfort of dogs, even for our eyes and ears and noses."

And the second dog spoke and he said, " We are more heedful of the arts. We bark at the moon more rhythmically than did our forefathers. And when we gaze at ourselves in the water we see that our features are clearer than the features of yesterday."

Then the third dog spoke and said, " But what interests me most and beguiles my mind is the tranquil understanding existing between dogdoms."

At that very moment they looked, and lo, the dog-catcher was approaching.

The three dogs sprang up and scampered down the street; and as they ran the third dog said, " For God's sake, run for your lives. Civilization is after us."

THE DANCER

Once there came to the court of the Prince of Birkasha a dancer with her musicians. And she was admitted to the court, and she danced before the prince to the music of the lute and the flute and the zither.

She danced the dance of flames, and the dance of swords and spears; she danced the dance of stars and the dance of space. And then she danced the dance of flowers in the wind.

After this she stood before the throne of the prince and bowed her body before him. And the prince bade her to come nearer, and he said unto her, " Beautiful woman, daughter of grace and delight, whence comes your art? And how is it that you command all the elements in your rhythms and your rhymes? "

And the dancer bowed again before the prince, and she answered, " Mighty and gracious Majesty, I know not the answer to your questionings. Only

this I know: The philosopher's soul dwells in his head, the poet's soul is in his heart; the singer's soul lingers about his throat, but the soul of the dancer abides in all her body."

THE TWO GUARDIAN ANGELS

On an evening two angels met at the city gate, and they greeted one another, and they conversed.

The one angel said, " What are you doing these days, and what work is given you? "

And the other answered, " It has been assigned me to be the guardian of a fallen man who lives down in the valley, a great sinner, most degraded. Let me assure you it is an important task, and I work hard."

The first angel said, " That is an easy commission. I have often known sinners, and have been their guardian many a time. But it has now been assigned me to be the guardian of the good saint who lives in a bower out yonder. And I assure you that is an exceedingly difficult work, and most subtle."

Said the first angel, " This is but assumption. How can guarding a saint be harder than guarding a sinner? "

And the other answered, "What impertinence, to call me assumptious! I have stated but the truth. Methinks it is you who are assumptious!"

Then the angels wrangled and fought, first with words and then with fists and wings.

While they were fighting an archangel came by. And he stopped them, and said, "Why do you fight? And what is it all about? Know you not that it is most unbecoming for guardian angels to fight at the city gate? Tell me, what is your disagreement?"

Then both angels spoke at once, each claiming that the work given him was the harder, and that he deserved the greater recognition.

The archangel shook his head and bethought him.

Then he said, "My friends, I cannot say now which one of you has the greater claim upon honor and reward. But since the power is bestowed in me, therefore for peace' sake and for good guardianship, I give to each of you the other's occupation, since each of you insists that the other's task is the easier one. Now go hence and be happy at your work."

The angels thus ordered went their ways. But each one looked backward with greater anger at the archangel. And in his heart each was saying, " Oh, these archangels! Every day they make life harder and still harder for us angels! "

But the archangel stood there, and once more he bethought him. And he said in his heart, " We have indeed, to be watchful and to keep guard over our guardian angels."

THE STATUE

Once there lived a man among the hills who possessed a statue wrought by an ancient master. It lay at his door face downward and he was not mindful of it.

One day there passed by his house a man from the city, a man of knowledge, and seeing the statue he inquired of the owner if he would sell it.

The owner laughed and said, " And pray who would want to buy that dull and dirty stone? "

The man from the city said, " I will give you this piece of silver for it."

And the other man was astonished and delighted.

The statue was removed to the city, upon the back of an elephant. And after many moons the man from the hills visited the city, and as he walked the streets he saw a crowd before a shop, and a man with a loud voice was crying, " Come ye in and behold the most beautiful, the most wonderful statue in all the world. Only two silver pieces to look upon this most marvelous work of a master."

Thereupon the man from the hills paid two silver pieces and entered the shop to see the statue that he himself had sold for one piece of silver.

THE EXCHANGE

Once upon a crossroad a poor Poet met a rich Stupid, and they conversed. And all that they said revealed but their discontent.

Then the Angel of the Road passed by, and he laid his hand upon the shoulder of the two men. And behold, a miracle: The two men had now exchanged their possessions.

And they parted. But strange to relate, the Poet looked and found naught in his hand but dry moving sand; and the Stupid closed his eyes and felt naught but moving cloud in his heart.

LOVE AND HATE

A woman said unto a man, " I love you." And the man said, " It is in my heart to be worthy of your love."

And the woman said, " You love me not? " And the man only gazed upon her and said nothing.

Then the woman cried aloud, " I hate you." And the man said, " Then it is also in my heart to be worthy of your hate."

DREAMS

A man dreamed a dream, and when he awoke he went to his soothsayer and desired that his dream be made plain unto him.

And the soothsayer said to the man, "Come to me with the dreams that you behold in your wakefulness and I will tell you their meaning. But the dreams of your sleep belong neither to my wisdom nor to your imagination."

THE MADMAN

It was in the garden of a madhouse that I met a youth with a face pale and lovely and full of wonder.

And I sat beside him upon the bench, and I said, " Why are you here? "

And he looked at me in astonishment, and he said, " It is an unseemly question, yet I will answer you. My father would make of me a reproduction of himself; so also would my uncle. My mother would have me the image of her illustrious father. My sister would hold up her seafaring husband as the perfect example for me to follow. My brother thinks I should be like him, a fine athlete.

" And my teachers also, the doctor of philosophy, and the music-master, and the logician, they too were determined, and each would have me but a reflection of his own face in a mirror.

"Therefore I came to this place. I find it more sane here. At least, I can be myself."

Then of a sudden he turned to me and he said, "But tell me, were you also driven to this place by education and good counsel?"

And I answered, "No, I am a visitor."

And he said, "Oh, you are one of those who live in the madhouse on the other side of the wall."

THE FROGS

Upon a summer day a frog said to his mate, " I fear those people living in that house on the shore are disturbed by our night-songs."

And his mate answered and said, " Well, do they not annoy our silence during the day with their talking? "

The frog said, " Let us not forget that we may sing too much in the night."

And his mate answered, " Let us not forget that they chatter and shout overmuch during the day."

Said the frog, " How about the bullfrog who disturbs the whole neighborhood with his God-forbidden booming? "

And his mate replied, " Aye, and what say you of the politician and the priest and the scientist who come to these shores and fill the air with noisy and rhymeless sound? "

Then the frog said, " Well, let us be better than

these human beings. Let us be quiet at night, and keep our songs in our hearts, even though the moon calls for our rhythm and the stars for our rhyme. At least, let us be silent for a night or two, or even for three nights."

And his mate said, " Very well, I agree. We shall see what your bountiful heart will bring forth."

That night the frogs were silent; and they were silent the following night also, and again upon the third night.

And strange to relate, the talkative woman who lived in the house beside the lake came down to breakfast on that third day and shouted to her husband, " I have not slept these three nights. I was secure with sleep when the noise of the frogs was in my ear. But something must have happened. They have not sung now for three nights; and I am almost maddened with sleeplessness."

The frog heard this and turned to his mate and said, winking his eye, " And we were almost maddened with our silence, were we not? "

And his mate answered, " Yes, the silence of

the night was heavy upon us. And I can see now that there is no need for us to cease our singing for the comfort of those who must needs fill their emptiness with noise."

And that night the moon called not in vain for their rhythm nor the stars for their rhyme.

LAWS AND LAW-GIVING

Ages ago there was a great king, and he was wise. And he desired to lay laws unto his subjects.

He called upon one thousand wise men of one thousand different tribes to come to his capitol and lay down the laws.

And all this came to pass.

But when the thousand laws written upon parchment were put before the king and he read them, he wept bitterly in his soul, for he had not known that there were one thousand forms of crime in his kingdom.

Then he called his scribe, and with a smile upon his mouth he himself dictated laws. And his laws were but seven.

And the one thousand wise men left him in anger and returned to their tribes with the laws they had laid down. And every tribe followed the laws of its wise men.

Therefore they have a thousand laws even to our own day.

It is a great country, but it has one thousand prisons, and the prisons are full of women and men, breakers of a thousand laws.

It is indeed a great country, but the people thereof are descendants of one thousand law-givers and of only one wise king.

YESTERDAY, TODAY AND TOMORROW

I said to my friend, " You see her leaning upon the arm of that man. It was but yesterday that she leaned thus upon my arm."

And my friend said, " And tomorrow she will lean upon mine."

I said, " Behold her sitting close at his side. It was but yesterday she sat close beside me."

And he answered, " Tomorrow she will sit beside me."

I said, " See, she drinks wine from his cup, and yesterday she drank from mine."

And he said, " Tomorrow, from my cup."

Then I said, " See how she gazes at him with love, and with yielding eyes. Yesterday she gazed thus upon me."

And my friend said, " It will be upon me she gazes tomorrow."

I said, " Do you not hear her now murmuring

songs of love into his ears? Those very songs of love she murmured but yesterday into my ears."

And my friend said, " And tomorrow she will murmur them in mine."

I said, " Why see, she is embracing him. It was but yesterday that she embraced me."

And my friend said, " She will embrace me tomorrow."

Then I said, " What a strange woman."

But he answered, " She is like unto life, possessed by all men; and like death, she conquers all men; and like eternity, she enfolds all men."

THE PHILOSOPHER AND THE
COBBLER

There came to a cobbler's shop a philosopher with worn shoes. And the philosopher said to the cobbler, " Please mend my shoes."

And the cobbler said, " I am mending another man's shoes now, and there are still other shoes to patch before I can come to yours. But leave your shoes here, and wear this other pair today, and come tomorrow for your own."

Then the philosopher was indignant, and he said, " I wear no shoes that are not mine own."

And the cobbler said, " Well then, are you in truth a philosopher, and cannot enfold your feet with the shoes of another man? Upon this very street there is another cobbler who understands philosophers better than I do. Go you to him for mending."

BUILDERS OF BRIDGES

In Antioch where the river Assi goes to meet the sea, a bridge was built to bring one half of the city nearer to the other half. It was built of large stones carried down from among the hills, on the backs of the mules of Antioch.

When the bridge was finished, upon a pillar thereof was engraven in Greek and in Aramaic, " This bridge was builded by King Antiochus II."

And all the people walked across the good bridge over the goodly river Assi.

And upon an evening, a youth, deemed by some a little mad, descended to the pillar where the words were engraven, and he covered over the graving with charcoal, and above it he wrote, " The stones of this bridge were brought down from the hills by the mules. In passing to and fro over it you are riding upon the backs of the mules of Antioch, builders of this bridge."

And when the people read what the youth had

written, some of them laughed and some marveled. And some said, " Ah yes, we know who has done this. Is he not a little mad? "

But one mule said, laughing, to another mule, " Do you not remember that we did carry those stones? And yet until now it has been said that the bridge was builded by King Antiochus."

THE FIELD OF ZAAD

Upon the road of Zaad a traveler met a man who lived in a nearby village, and the traveler, pointing with his hand to a vast field, asked the man saying, " Was not this the battle-ground where King Ahlam overcame his enemies? "

And the man answered and said, " This has never been a battle-ground. There once stood on this field the great city of Zaad, and it was burnt down to ashes. But now it is a good field, is it not? "

And the traveler and the man parted.

Not a half mile farther the traveler met another man, and pointing to the field again, he said, " So that is where the great city of Zaad once stood? "

And the man said, " There has never been a city in this place. But once there was a monastery here, and it was destroyed by the people of the South Country."

Shortly after, on that very road of Zaad, the

traveler met a third man, and pointing once more to the vast field he said, " Is it not true that this is the place where once there stood a great monastery? "

But the man answered, " There has never been a monastery in this neighborhood, but our fathers and our forefathers have told us that once there fell a great meteor on this field."

Then the traveler walked on, wondering in his heart. And he met a very old man, and saluting him he said, " Sir, upon this road I have met three men who live in the neighborhood and I have asked each of them about this field, and each one denied what the other had said, and each one told me a new tale that the other had not told."

Then the old man raised his head, and answered, " My friend, each and every one of these men told you what was indeed so; but few of us are able to add fact to different fact and make a truth thereof."

THE GOLDEN BELT

Once upon a day two men who met on the road were walking together toward Salamis, the City of Columns. In mid-afternoon they came to a wide river and there was no bridge to cross it. They must needs swim, or seek another road unknown to them.

And they said to one another, " Let us swim. After all, the river is not so wide." And they threw themselves into the water and swam.

And one of the men who had always known rivers and the ways of rivers, in mid-stream suddenly began to lose himself, and to be carried away by the rushing waters; while the other who had never swum before crossed the river straightway and stood upon the farther bank. Then seeing his companion still wrestling with the stream, he threw himself again into the waters and brought him also safely to the shore.

And the man who had been swept away by

the current said, " But you told me you could not swim. How then did you cross that river with such assurance? "

And the second man answered, " My friend, do you see this belt which girdles me? It is full of golden coins that I have earned for my wife and my children, a full year's work. It is the weight of this belt of gold that carried me across the river, to my wife and my children. And my wife and my children were upon my shoulders as I swam."

And the two men walked on together toward Salamis.

THE RED EARTH

Said a tree to a man, " My roots are in the deep red earth, and I shall give you of my fruit."

And the man said to the tree, " How alike we are. My roots are also deep in the red earth. And the red earth gives you power to bestow upon me of your fruit, and the red earth teaches me to receive from you with thanksgiving."

THE FULL MOON

The full moon rose in glory upon the town, and all the dogs of that town began to bark at the moon.

Only one dog did not bark, and he said to them in a grave voice, " Awake not stillness from her sleep, nor bring you the moon to the earth with your barking."

Then all the dogs ceased barking, in awful silence. But the dog who had spoken to them continued barking for silence, the rest of the night.

THE HERMIT PROPHET

Once there lived a hermit prophet, and thrice a moon he would go down to the great city and in the market places he would preach giving and sharing to the people. And he was eloquent, and his fame was upon the land.

Upon an evening three men came to his hermitage and he greeted them. And they said, " You have been preaching giving and sharing, and you have sought to teach those who have much to give unto those who have little; and we doubt not that your fame has brought you riches. Now come and give us of your riches, for we are in need."

And the hermit answered and said, " My friends, I have naught but this bed and this mat and this jug of water. Take them if it is in your desire. I have neither gold nor silver."

Then they looked down with disdain upon him, and turned their faces from him; and the last man stood at the door for a moment, and said, " Oh, you cheat! You fraud! You teach and preach that which you yourself do not perform."

THE OLD, OLD WINE

Once there lived a rich man who was justly proud of his cellar and the wine therein. And there was one jug of ancient vintage kept for some occasion known only to himself.

The governor of the state visited him, and he bethought him and said, " That jug shall not be opened for a mere governor."

And a bishop of the diocese visited him, but he said to himself, " Nay, I will not open that jug. He would not know its value, nor would its aroma reach his nostrils."

The prince of the realm came and supped with him. But he thought, " It is too royal a wine for a mere princeling."

And even on the day when his own nephew was married, he said to himself, " No, not to these guests shall that jug be brought forth."

And the years passed by, and he died, an old

man, and he was buried like unto every seed and acorn.

And upon the day that he was buried the ancient jug was brought out together with other jugs of wine, and it was shared by the peasants of the neighborhood. And none knew its great age.

To them, all that is poured into a cup is only wine.

THE TWO POEMS

Many centuries ago, on a road to Athens, two poets met, and they were glad to see one another.

And one poet asked the other saying, " What have you composed of late, and how goes it with your lyre? "

And the other poet answered and said with pride, " I have but now finished the greatest of my poems, perchance the greatest poem yet written in Greek. It is an invocation to Zeus the Supreme."

Then he took from beneath his cloak a parchment, saying, " Here, behold, I have it with me, and I would fain read it to you. Come, let us sit in the shade of that white cypress."

And the poet read his poem. And it was a long poem.

And the other poet said in kindliness, " This is a great poem. It will live through the ages, and in it you shall be glorified."

And the first poet said calmly, " And what have you been writing these late days? "

And the other answered, " I have written but little. Only eight lines in remembrance of a child playing in a garden." And he recited the lines.

The first poet said, " Not so bad; not so bad."

And they parted.

And now after two thousand years the eight lines of the one poet are read in every tongue, and are loved and cherished.

And though the other poem has indeed come down through the ages in libraries and in the cells of scholars, and though it is remembered, it is neither loved nor read.

LADY RUTH

Three men once looked from afar upon a white house that stood alone on a green hill. One of them said, " That is the house of Lady Ruth. She is an old witch."

The second man said, " You are wrong. Lady Ruth is a beautiful woman who lives there consecrated unto her dreams."

The third man said, " You are both wrong. Lady Ruth is the holder of this vast land, and she draws blood from her serfs."

And they walked on discussing Lady Ruth.

Then when they came to a crossroad they met an old man, and one of them asked him, saying, " Would you please tell us about Lady Ruth who lives in that white house upon the hill? "

And the old man raised his head and smiled upon them, and said, " I am ninety of years, and I remember Lady Ruth when I was but

66

a boy. But Lady Ruth died eighty years ago, and now the house is empty. The owls hoot therein, sometimes, and people say the place is haunted."

THE MOUSE AND THE CAT

Once on an evening a poet met a peasant. The poet was distant and the peasant was shy, yet they conversed.

And the peasant said, " Let me tell you a little story which I heard of late. A mouse was caught in a trap, and while he was happily eating the cheese that lay therein, a cat stood by. The mouse trembled awhile, but he knew he was safe within the trap.

" Then the cat said, ' You are eating your last meal, my friend.'

" ' Yes,' answered the mouse, ' one life have I, therefore one death. But what of you? They tell me you have nine lives. Doesn't that mean that you will have to die nine times? ' "

And the peasant looked at the poet and he said, " Is not this a strange story? "

And the poet answered him not, but he walked away saying in his soul, " To be sure, nine lives have we, nine lives to be sure. And we shall die nine times, nine times shall we die. Perhaps it were better to have but one life, caught in a trap — the life of a peasant with a bit of cheese for the last meal. And yet, are we not kin unto the lions of the desert and the jungle? "

THE CURSE

An old man of the sea once said to me, " It was thirty years ago that a sailor ran away with my daughter. And I cursed them both in my heart, for of all the world I loved but my daughter.

" Not long after that, the sailor youth went down with his ship to the bottom of the sea, and with him my lovely daughter was lost unto me.

" Now therefore behold in me the murderer of a youth and a maid. It was my curse that destroyed them. And now on my way to the grave I seek God's forgiveness."

This the old man said. But there was a tone of bragging in his words, and it seems that he is still proud of the power of his curse.

THE POMEGRANATES

There was once a man who had many pomegranate trees in his orchard. And for many an autumn he would put his pomegranates on silvery trays outside of his dwelling, and upon the trays he would place signs upon which he himself had written, " Take one for aught. You are welcome."

But people passed by and no one took of the fruit.

Then the man bethought him, and one autumn he placed no pomegranates on silvery trays outside of his dwelling, but he raised this sign in large lettering: " Here we have the best pomegranates in the land, but we sell them for more silver than any other pomegranates."

And now behold, all the men and women of the neighborhood came rushing to buy.

GOD AND MANY GODS

In the city of Kilafis a sophist stood on the steps of the Temple and preached many gods. And the people said in their hearts, " We know all this. Do they not live with us and follow us wherever we go? "

Not long after, another man stood in the market place and spoke unto the people and said, " There is no god." And many who heard him were glad of his tidings, for they were afraid of gods.

And upon another day there came a man of great eloquence, and he said, " There is but one God." And now the poeple were dismayed for in their hearts they feared the judgment of one God more than that of many gods.

That same season there came yet another man, and he said to the people, " There are three gods, and they dwell upon the wind as one, and they have a vast and gracious mother who is also their mate and their sister."

Then everyone was comforted, for they said in their secret, " Three gods in one must needs disagree over our failings, and besides, their gracious mother will surely be an advocate for us poor weaklings."

Yet even to this day there are those in the city of Kilafis who wrangle and argue with each other about many gods and no god, and one god and three gods in one, and a gracious mother of gods.

SHE WHO WAS DEAF

Once there lived a rich man who had a young wife, and she was stone deaf.

And upon a morning when they were breaking their fast, she spoke to him and she said, " Yesterday I visited the market place, and there were exhibited silken raiment from Damascus, and coverchiefs from India, necklaces from Persia, and bracelets from Yamman. It seems that the caravans had but just brought these things to our city. And now behold me, in rags, yet the wife of a rich man. I would have some of those beautiful things."

The husband, still busy with his morning coffee said, " My dear, there is *no* reason why you should not go down to the Street and buy all that your heart may desire."

And the deaf wife said, " ' *No!* ' You always say, ' No, no.' Must I needs appear in tatters among our friends to shame your wealth and my people? "

And the husband said, " I did not say, ' *No.*' You may go forth freely to the market place and purchase the most beautiful apparel and jewels that have come to our city."

But again the wife mis-read his words, and she replied, " Of all rich men you are the most miserly. You would deny me everything of beauty and loveliness, while other women of my age walk the gardens of the city clothed in rich raiment."

And she began to weep. And as her tears fell upon her breast she cried out again, " You always say, ' Nay, nay ' to me when I desire a garment or a jewel."

Then the husband was moved, and he stood up and took out of his purse a handful of gold and placed it before her, saying in a kindly voice, " Go down to the market place, my dear, and buy all that you will."

From that day onward the deaf young wife, whenever she desired anything, would appear before her husband with a pearly tear in her eye, and he in silence would take out a handful of gold and place it in her lap.

Now, it chanced that the young woman fell in love with a youth whose habit it was to make long journeys. And whenever he was away she would sit in her casement and weep.

When her husband found her thus weeping, he would say in his heart, " There must be some new caravan, and some silken garments and rare jewels in the Street."

And he would take a handful of gold and place it before her.

THE QUEST

A thousand years ago two philosophers met on a slope of Lebanon, and one said to the other, " Where goest thou? "

And the other answered, " I am seeking after the fountain of youth which I know wells out among these hills. I have found writings which tell of that fountain flowering toward the sun. And you, what are you seeking? "

The first man answered, " I am seeking after the mystery of death."

Then each of the two philosophers conceived that the other was lacking in his great science, and they began to wrangle, and to accuse each other of spiritual blindness.

Now while the two philosophers were loud upon the wind, a stranger, a man who was deemed a simpleton in his own village, passed by, and when he heard the two in hot dispute, he stood awhile and listened to their argument.

Then he came near to them and said, " My good men, it seems that you both really belong to the same school of philosophy, and that you are speaking of the same thing, only you speak in different words. One of you seeks the fountain of youth, and the other seeks the mystery of death. Yet indeed they are but one, and as one they dwell in you both."

Then the stranger turned away saying, " Farewell, sages." And as he departed he laughed a patient laughter.

The two philosophers looked at each other in silence for a moment, and then they laughed also. And one of them said, " Well now, shall we not walk and seek together? "

THE SCEPTRE

Said a king to his wife, " Madame, you are not truly a queen. You are too vulgar and ungracious to be my mate."

Said his wife, " Sir, you deem yourself king, but indeed you are only a poor soundling."

Now these words angered the king, and he took his sceptre with his hand, and struck the queen upon her forehead with his golden sceptre.

At that moment the lord chamberlain entered, and he said, " Well, well, Majesty! That sceptre was fashioned by the greatest artist of the land. Alas! Some day you and the queen shall be forgotten, but this sceptre shall be kept, a thing of beauty from generation to generation. And now that you have drawn blood from her Majesty's head, Sire, the sceptre shall be the more considered and remembered."

THE PATH

There lived among the hills a woman and her son, and he was her first-born and her only child.

And the boy died of a fever whilst the physician stood by.

The mother was distraught with sorrow, and she cried to the physician and besought him saying, " Tell me, tell me, what was it that made quiet his striving and silent his song? "

And the physician said, " It was the fever."

And the mother said, " What is the fever? "

And the physician answered, " I cannot explain it. It is a thing infinitely small that visits the body, and we cannot see it with our human eye."

Then the physician left her. And she kept repeating to herself, " something infinitely small. We cannot see it with our human eye."

And at evening the priest came to console her. And she wept and she cried out saying, " Oh, why have I lost my son, my only son, my first-born? "

And the priest answered, " My child, it is the will of God."

And the woman said, " What is God and where is God? I would see God that I may tear my bosom before Him, and pour the blood of my heart at His feet. Tell me where I shall find Him."

And the priest said, " God is infinitely vast. He is not to be seen with our human eye."

Then the woman cried out, " The infinitely small has slain my son through the will of the infinitely great! Then what are we? What are we? "

At that moment the woman's mother came into the room with the shroud for the dead boy, and she heard the words of the priest and also her daughter's cry. And she laid down the shroud, and took her daughter's hand in her own hand, and she said, " My daughter, we ourselves are the infinitely small and the infinitely great; and we are the path between the two."

THE WHALE
AND THE BUTTERFLY

Once on an evening a man and a woman found themselves together in a stagecoach. They had met before.

The man was a poet, and as he sat beside the woman he sought to amuse her with stories, some that were of his own weaving, and some that were not his own.

But even while he was speaking the lady went to sleep. Then suddenly the coach lurched, and she awoke, and she said, " I admire your interpretation of the story of Jonah and the whale."

And the poet said, " But Madame, I have been telling you a story of mine own about a butterfly and a white rose, and how they behaved the one to the other! "

PEACE CONTAGIOUS

One branch in bloom said to his neighboring branch, " This is a dull and empty day." And the other branch answered, " It is indeed empty and dull."

At that moment a sparrow alighted on one of the branches, and then another sparrow, nearby.

And one of the sparrows chirped and said, " My mate has left me."

And the other sparrow cried, " My mate has also gone, and she will not return. And what care I? "

Then the two began to twitter and scold, and soon they were fighting and making harsh noise upon the air.

All of a sudden two other sparrows came sailing from the sky, and they sat quietly beside the restless two. And there was calm, and there was peace.

Then the four flew away together in pairs.

And the first branch said to his neighboring branch, " That was a mighty zig-zag of sound." And the other branch answered, " Call it what you will, it is now both peaceful and spacious. And if the upper air makes peace it seems to me that those who dwell in the lower might make peace also. Will you not wave in the wind a little nearer to me? "

And the first branch said, " Oh, perchance, for peace' sake, ere the Spring is over."

And then he waved himself with the strong wind to embrace her.

THE SHADOW

Upon a June day the grass said to the shadow of an elm tree, " You move to right and left over-often, and you disturb my peace."

And the shadow answered and said, " Not I, not I. Look skyward. There is a tree that moves in the wind to the east and to the west, between the sun and the earth."

And the grass looked up, and for the first time beheld the tree. And it said in its heart, " Why, behold, there is a larger grass than myself."

And the grass was silent.

SEVENTY

The poet youth said to the princess, " I love you." And the princess answered, " And I love you too, my child."

" But I am not your child. I am a man and I love you."

And she said, " I am the mother of sons and daughters, and they are fathers and mothers of sons and daughters; and one of the sons of my sons is older than you."

And the poet youth said, " But I love you."

It was not long after that the princess died. But ere her last breath was received again by the greater breath of earth, she said within her soul, " My beloved, mine only son, my youth-poet, it may yet be that some day we shall meet again, and I shall not be seventy."

FINDING GOD

Two men were walking in the valley, and one man pointed with his finger toward the mountain side, and said, " See you that hermitage? There lives a man who has long divorced the world. He seeks but after God, and naught else upon this earth."

And the other man said, " He shall not find God until he leaves his hermitage, and the aloneness of his hermitage, and returns to our world, to share our joy and pain, to dance with our dancers at the wedding feast, and to weep with those who weep around the coffins of our dead."

And the other man was convinced in his heart, though in spite of his conviction he answered, " I agree with all that you say, yet I believe the hermit is a good man. And may it not well be that one good man by his absence does better than the seeming goodness of these many men? "

87

THE RIVER

In the valley of Kadisha where the mighty river flows, two little streams met and spoke to one another.

One stream said, " How came you, my friend, and how was your path? "

And the other answered, " My path was most encumbered. The wheel of the mill was broken, and the master farmer who used to conduct me from my channel to his plants, is dead. I struggled down oozing with the filth of those who do naught but sit and bake their laziness in the sun. But how was your path, my brother? "

And the other stream answered and said, " Mine was a different path. I came down the hills among fragrant flowers and shy willows; men and women drank of me with silvery cups, and little children paddled their rosy feet at my edges, and there was laughter all about me, and there were sweet songs. What a pity that your path was not so happy."

At that moment the river spoke with a loud voice and said, " Come in, come in, we are going to the sea. Come in, come in, speak no more. Be with me now. We are going to the sea. Come in, come in, for in me you shall forget your wanderings, sad or gay. Come in, come in. And you and I will forget all our ways when we reach the heart of our mother the sea."

THE TWO HUNTERS

Upon a day in May, Joy and Sorrow met beside a lake. They greeted one another, and they sat down near the quiet waters and conversed.

Joy spoke of the beauty which is upon the earth, and of the daily wonder of life in the forest and among the hills, and of the songs heard at dawn and eventide.

And Sorrow spoke, and agreed with all that Joy had said; for Sorrow knew the magic of the hour and the beauty thereof. And Sorrow was eloquent when he spoke of May in the fields and among the hills.

And Joy and Sorrow talked long together, and they agreed upon all things of which they knew.

Now there passed by on the other side of the lake two hunters. And as they looked across the water one of them said, " I wonder who are those two persons? " And the other said, " Did you say two? I see only one."

90

The first hunter said, " But there are two." And the second said, " There is only one that I can see, and the reflection in the lake is only one."

" Nay, there are two," said the first hunter, " and the reflection in the still water is of two persons."

But the second man said again, " Only one do I see." And again the other said, " But I see two so plainly."

And even to this day one hunter says that the other sees double; while the other says, " My friend is somewhat blind."

THE OTHER WANDERER

Once on a time I met another man of the roads. He too was a little mad, and thus he spoke to me: "I am a wanderer. Oftentimes it seems that I walk the earth among pygmies. And because my head is seventy cubits farther from the earth than theirs, it creates higher and freer thoughts.

"But in truth I walk not among men but above them, and all they can see of me is my footprints in their open fields.

"And often have I heard them discuss and disagree over the shape and size of my footprints. For there are some who say, 'These are the tracks of a mammoth that roamed the earth in the far past.' And others say, 'Nay, these are places where meteors have fallen from the distant stars.'

"But you, my friend, you know full well that they are naught save the footprints of a wanderer."

PRINTER'S NOTE

This book was set on the Linotype in GRANJON, *a type named in compliment to Robert Granjon, type-cutter and printer — 1523–1590, Antwerp, Lyons, Rome, Paris. Granjon, the boldest and most original designer of his time, was one of the first to practice the trade of type-founder apart from that of printer.*

Linotype GRANJON *was designed by George W. Jones, who based his drawings upon a face used by Claude Garamond (1510–1561) in his beautiful French books.* GRANJON *more closely resembles Garamond's own type than do any of the various modern faces that bear his name.*

PRINTED AND BOUND BY THE BOOK PRESS,

BRATTLEBORO, VERMONT.